Joanne was born in 1971 in the
loved writing and sharing her s
and family. Add into her life twenty-five years with her husband
and soulmate as well as a global move to Australia and you have
all the inspiration that you need. She has recently completed a
diploma in professional writing and has commenced work on her
first novel.

For my husband, Mark.
For my mum and dad.

Joanne Hattersley

Ramblings of a Forty-Something Widow

Austin Macauley Publishers™

LONDON • CAMBRIDGE • NEW YORK • SHARJAH

Copyright © Joanne Hattersley (2020)

The right of Joanne Hattersley to be identified as author of this work has been asserted by the author in accordance with section 77 and 78 of the Copyright, Designs and Patents Act 1988.

All rights reserved. No part of this publication may be reproduced, stored in a retrieval system, or transmitted in any form or by any means, electronic, mechanical, photocopying, recording, or otherwise, without the prior permission of the publishers.

Any person who commits any unauthorised act in relation to this publication may be liable to criminal prosecution and civil claims for damages.

Austin Macauley is committed to publishing works of quality and integrity. In this spirit, we are proud to offer this book to our readers; however, the story, the experiences, and the words are the author's alone.

A CIP catalogue record for this title is available from the British Library.

ISBN 9781398403321 (Paperback)
ISBN 9781398403338 (ePub e-book)

www.austinmacauley.com

First Published (2020)
Austin Macauley Publishers Ltd
25 Canada Square
Canary Wharf
London
E14 5LQ

Mark, my husband. Even though you are no longer with me in person, your endless love, support and laughter through life always ensured that I knew I was on the right track. You were my biggest fan. You gave me the confidence to believe in myself and chase my dreams. I love you.

To Mum and Dad. Your love and support is beautiful and unconditional. Thank you for loving me, caring for me and displaying my work in your house!

To my brother, Lee, and sister-in-law, Clare. For every memory we shared with Mark. For every late-night chat, drink and laughter we shared after Mark. For your love, kindness and just for being you.

Matthew and Charlotte, thank you for being in my life. Thank you for loving me and being there after the loss of your dad. Despite your own grief, you made sure that I was fine too.

Sheila, I could not wish for a more supportive mother in law. You love me as a daughter and see me as a friend. We have shared valuable memories with Mark and as just us girls together. Thank you for your love.

Kevin and Michael, two brothers-in-law that have accepted me as a sister. Thank you for your support.

Thank you, Des, Martin, Tony and Tracey. Not only did you inspire me with support and your six-day trip to Australia but you are best friends. Thank you for being on the end of a phone when I need you.

Thank you, Susie, for your kind support, love and laughter. Thank you for allowing me to bounce ideas with you.

Nathan, thank you for ideas through my course. Your imagination far exceeds your ten years of life. You are a constant source of fun and entertainment. Love you, buddy.

A special mention to John, Caroline, Alan and Elaine. You have known me since the day I was born and have been friends that have become family. I can't imagine not having you in my life.

Foreword

I met Joanne on the 25th of December, 1971, just a few hours after she was born. You would expect a baby born at 7am on Christmas morning to bring something special to the world, but at the time it was enough to have ten fingers and ten toes. Yes, I'm Barry Beckham, Joanne's Dad, so I may have just a tiny bias. Here we are, 49 years later, I've been asked to write a foreword for her first book.

When musicians who have penned and recorded great music, are asked to explain what the inspiration was, it seems that it often came from one or more of life's adversities. From sadness springs creativity, it seems. The author of this work has had enough of life's adversities, first choosing to work in the health service and for many years with dementia patients.

In recent times, she has provided a number of years' care to her own husband who was suffering from myasthenia gravis. He lost his battle in 2019 and it's that adversity that has impacted Joanne within her poems and words. As this work is published, the twenty-four-hour care she gave her husband seamlessly switched to her mother, who has terminal cancer.

As a child, she loved writing and sharing her stories and poems with her friends and family, but if life's adversity does bring out the best in us then this work is it. Through all her trials of life, I've never seen that burden adversely shown on the surface and that old saying comes to mind about a swan. All serene and dignified on the surface, but frantic paddling beneath the water to keep afloat.

These poems are her paddling, but rather than frantic, they are calming, perhaps a little sad at times, especially if you have also experienced a loss of someone close. Rather than allow herself to become overwhelmed, Joanne has poured her emotions into her writing and that is an inspirational thing to do and something she continues to this day.

Yes, I'm her dad, so I'm just a little biased, which means you have to read her work and make up your own mind. Her writing has blossomed into a new chapter in her life, she's passionate about it. So, read on and help her reach that next chapter. Keep turning the pages.

– Barry Beckham

Poem 1
Myasthenia Gravis

When MG came a-calling,
It knocked so very hard.
We didn't have much warning,
It left us feeling scarred.

The neuro did a check,
Take these pills he said.
Let me know about your eyesight,
It left us with some dread.

The double vision left him,
About twenty minutes in.
We thought it was a miracle,
Signs started to begin.

Double vision came and went,
As meds were given timely.
Yet there was still more to come,
We started to think wisely.

Add into this, weakened limbs,
Inability to stand,
Also, throw in breathing bad,
None of this was planned.

Could have said why is this us
That it has happened to.
Could have said why is this us?

Oh, little that we knew.

Start to chuck in treatments,
Injections and the meds.
Throw in blood tests regularly,
Can tear your life to shreds.

Lots more treatments came and went,
Nothing seemed to fit.
Hospitals were the second home,
But still we wouldn't quit.

There was the time in ICU
As scary as all hell.
They wouldn't allow him home to me,
Until he was all well.

Add on severe infection,
Throw in a blood clot too.
The time we spent in hospital,
It grew and grew and grew.

Now we're making memories,
Enjoying life to come.
Don't know how much he has left,
It's not as long as some.

Limited time is all we have,
Memories to make.
Silver wedding coming up,
We'll have to get a cake.

Visitors are coming,
Best friends of my man.
Flying all way round the world,
Will fun begin? It can.

So onwards upwards we will go.
No point that we should fret.
We still have each other
And memories to get.

Poem 2
25th Wedding Celebrations

In 1993 you said,
How about you marry me.
I didn't have to think for long.
The rest is history.

In 1994, we wed.
We shared our special day.
Didn't need the fancy wedding stuff.
I do, I heard you say.

We started life together.
Made many memories.
Helping to raise the kids.
Life was good you see.

Throughout the years, we went away.
Ibiza, Turkey too.
Then we tried America,
A new world for me and you.

We worked so hard to pay the bills.
Moved out to a nice house,
Much more space, a garden too.
This great life with my spouse.

I can count the memories,
There are heaps and heaps.
How do you choose a favourite one?
All of them I can keep.

We worked so hard, eventually,
Moved to The Land of Oz.
Change of lifestyle what we want,
Want life to take a pause.

Time off together we found we had,
Not for a long, long time.
All the while we worked,
Raising money for our life.

We found we loved the country,
Green and gold the colours were.
Still love the fact we're British,
But Australia now called home.

Roll on and years have passed now.
This year 25 years wed.
What an achievement we have made.
Let's love the years ahead.

Poem 3
Christmas

We had a great Christmas, the family together.
The memories made, all through that day.
The turkey is on, roast potatoes are cooking.
Pour me a glass. I'll have Cabernet.

The time is approaching, must serve it all up now.
My mum steps right in to do what she there for.
With the meal and the booze we go right ahead feeding.
We all eat and drink, keep going some more.

When dinner is done, the plates to the kitchen,
Dishwasher open and stack it I do.
Switch the thing on and back to the drinking,
My glass of Prosecco is poured out by you.

Later, my dad finds the whiskey bottle.
Comes over to Mark and pours him a glass.
Goes back again, there is more there to have now.
Lagavulin – now that's what you call class.

We head to the TV and find a crap movie.
At Christmas, there is nothing decent that's on.
Let's find a Blu-ray to watch, my dad says to us.
All had a choice. Birthday girl won.

We find Monty Python, a laugh we will have now.
Remembering all the old sketches we knew.
Still seem so funny, even all these years later.
Old memories seem to always ring true.

Thinking of headaches we'll all have tomorrow.
Not worrying now as there isn't much point.
We laughed, smiled, eaten and drunk.
Carrying on with not a single complaint.

Thank you for the memories
That you have given me.
Forty-seven years of them,
As precious as can be.

Poem 4
Left Behind

Eating at weird times,
Crying when I'm sad.
Wondering why you left me,
It makes me bloody mad.

I know your time was over,
We both did, said goodbye.
I told you I'd be fine now,
You knew it was a lie.

You knew I'd be heartbroken,
Living without you.
You knew I'd struggle coping,
You knew it was hard too.

Wanted you here forever.
No possibility.
Myasthenia put paid to that.
That awfully bad disease.

It feels like you're still here now,
Lying in that room.
Waiting for you to call for me,
I know it won't happen soon.

Remembering you're gone now,
The pain is agony.
You were my friend, my soulmate,
The only one for me.

I miss you more than anything.
Your voice, your face, your laugh.
I miss you sitting with me.
I miss hearing you talk.

My life has changed so much now,
Don't know what to think.
Every memory sitting there,
New ones every time I blink.

Thank you for the travel.
Thank you for the fun.
Thank you for Australia.
Now all is said and done.

I know I must move forward,
Time is what it'll take.
I know I must move forward,
Someday when I wake.

Poem 5
Memories from Childhood...

The door opened
With a shove.
The light on,
This room I love.

The room from childhood,
When I was small.
The room with memories,
Come one and all.

Remember sleeping,
On my small bed.
Shared with my brother,
It's here we read.

Read books together,
Ladybirds they were.
The Magic porridge pot
And Cinderella.

There were so many.
The gingerbread man.
But one was special
For the memories it had.

Called Chicken Licken,
Made my brother laugh.
All the characters,
In each paragraph.

Chicken Licken,
Foxy too,
It made him giggle
As I read through.

Ducky Lucky,
Turkey Too,
Nicknamed him lurkey
As I read through.

Henry Penny
Joined the fun.
With Drakey Lakey,
This book's not done.

Goosey Loosey
Was there as well
So was Gander Lander
In the book, I tell.

I won't tell the end,
Will spoil it, it may.
Suffice to say,
You should read this one day.

Poem 6
Thanks Mum

Thank you for raising a daughter,
Thank you for raising a friend,
Thank you for all of our memories,
From the start of our lives till the end.

I know that our lives are not over
And neither should they be,
There is so much more to be crammed in,
Much more for you and for me.

Thank you for all of our lunches,
In all of the places we have been.
Early days was BHS stores,
You me and Nan, we were keen.

Memories walking round Romford,
Memories shopping with you,
Memories walking the market,
There was so much that we could do.

Memories chatting on the phone,
Memories sitting with you,
Memories sitting at dinner,
Sometimes with dad or both of you.

Memories all of my birthdays,
Ours were just a week apart.
Memories of our birthday lunches,
Tradition we decided to start.

Every memory with you is so precious.
Those memories are just you and me.
You're my mum and I am your daughter,
Of that I think we'd agree.

Poem 7
Mum and Dad...
Memories Together

Numbers are just numbers. It's the memories you share.
The little things you've said and done. The what and why and where.

In 1970, you said I do. The rest is history.
In '71, a girl called Joanne, '77 a boy called Lee.

You stayed at home, Mum, raised us kids. There every day for us.
Saw us off to school and then saw us back home, no fuss.

Dad was off and working hard. Making us a life.
Father to his children and devoted to his wife.

You took us away for holidays and showed us all around.
Cornwall, Wales and Scotland. But The Lakes, our favourite ground.

Memories of those holidays. Me grounding out the boat.
The dead man in Lake Coniston…that story scared us most.

Memories of the Lakeside steamer and Haverthwaite railway.
Putting coins upon the track to flatten for that day.

I still have my coins from there. These memories safely stored.
The best days I had in my life, my family, the Beckham horde.

You both supported us as we grew. Supported us through life.
Supported me as I found a husband and Lee a fiancé/wife.

Supported me throughout family of my own and Lee having his kid.
I had a boy, I had a girl. Lee had his Mitsubishi.

No matter what we talk about, it's there in front of me.
A dad and mum who love their kids, clear for the world to see.

We celebrate the two of you, a husband and a wife,
And your memories you have had, all throughout your life.

Poem 8
The Beach

Watching the sea roll into the shore,
The sand is disappearing some more.
Clouds are floating across the sky,
The sun is streaming into my eyes.

The sea looking threatening, waves crashing below,
Luckily, no boats. There is nowhere to go.
Nice and warm, I'm watching from here,
This view never tires. Year after year.

As the seasons move through, I'm outside now,
The weathers warming, sun across the bow.
Kick off my shoes as I get to the sand,
Running quickly, the beach is where I land.

Feeling the sand beneath my feet,
Not a clue who I might meet.
Man with a dog, kids playing below,
Anyone I see says hello.

Life passes by as I stand there,
Watching everyone without a care.
Not knowing what my plans will be,
As I stand there staring at the sea.

Looking up, the clouds roll in,
Hearing thunder, what a din.
Running now to escape the rain,
Maybe later I'll go out again.

Poem 9
Miss you, Hubby

Looking at your pictures
Still cannot quite believe
That you're never coming home
That you had to leave.

I know your time was over.
We both knew it was soon.
It just never seemed that fair to us.
We thought we could be immune.

But that time is here now.
I'm left here, now just me.
Looking at your photographs.
Just memories to see.

The house has hints of you here,
Scattered all around.
Everywhere I look, there is
Something to be found.

I miss your voice each morning,
I miss it late at night,
I miss our late night chats we had,
Always such a delight.

I miss your hugs and kisses,
I miss your hand to hold,
I miss the words you said to me
That no one else was told.

I miss the life together.
Breakfast out with you.
I miss the rugby games nights
We only got a few.

I miss cooking you dinner.
I miss sharing wine.
I miss going to the cinema.
I miss that you were mine.

I'm sad that you're not here now.
It feels like it's been years.
My life feels very empty.
Had my fair share of tears.

Life will change, move forward,
Of that I am very sure.
One things for sure, my memories of you
Will stay so very secure.

Poem 10
Life

Slide in, screaming, crying,
Time just goes so fast.
It's what you do in between,
That legacy will last.

You start at home with family,
Moving on to go to school.
Making friends, both boys and girls,
Together play the fool.

Those friends will last forever,
At least that's what you hope.
Some may come and some may go,
That you'll never know.

Learning facts at school,
These years go on and on.
Seeming like they'll never end,
All too quick they're gone.

Moving to a job now.
What do I want to do?
Choices now I have to make.
I have to think it through.

Meet the love of my life.
Time for me to wed.
Can't imagine life without him,
He's always in my head.

Memories we made together,
Holidays overseas,
Buying our first house as a couple,
Life becomes a breeze.

Spending time together,
More than we'd ever done.
Loving every second,
It's as if we're one.

Life moves on in memories,
Things we've said and done.
Thinking about it all now,
We had a lot of fun.

Life can throw a curveball,
Straight at you who knows when.
When it does, you catch it,
Deal with what comes next.

Myasthenia was our curveball,
The illness hit us hard.
Didn't see that coming,
Left us feeling scarred.

Bad eyes hit him first.
Weak muscles came on next.
Soon he had to quit work.
We both were feeling vexed.

Symptoms came and added up.
More and more and more.
We know we have to deal with it,
Please don't give us any more.

So life continues on for us.
Just have to get up, move on.
Life can be short, don't waste it.
Before you know it, it's gone.

Poem 11
Just You...

I never thought that I would be
Married at 22.
I never thought that I would find
An amazing man like you.

You took me under your wing and said,
Now will you marry me?
You were standing on a railway line
And wouldn't move you see.

I said yes and we got wed.
I would never change a thing.
Who needs the fancy wedding stuff?
Who knew what life would bring.

You are the man that I adore.
There's only one of you.
Exclusivity I am glad.
Nothing else will do.

You've shown me places round the world.
You've shown me how to cook.
You've shown me how to travel around
Our land to take a look.

You've made me into the woman
That I am proud to be.
You've made me feel so wonderful
That is plain to see.

I'm proud to be beside you.
I'm proud to call you mine.
I'm proud to call you husband.
I'm proud I am your wife.

Poem 12
Fathers and Daughters

The first man in a girl's life,
That man is her dad.
No one measures up to him.
No one ever can.

He's everything she's looking for.
He shows her all the world.
He tells her jokes and stories.
He makes her whole life whole.

No matter where life takes her,
Her dad is always there.
He always will support her.
You'll find he always cares.

He will be there at her school days.
He's there when she gets wed.
He's there to see a new house.
As she forges life ahead.

No matter what her age is.
No matter where she is.
She'll always be his little girl.
He'll always be her dad.

Poem 13
Sally

Funny stories she would tell,
I still have me some of those.
Read them again occasionally,
Her words they flowed and flowed.

She always was a favourite,
Always there for me.
My daddy's youngest sister,
A confidante you'll see.

Sent me letters, gifts and cards,
All the time we lived apart.
Earrings, clothes and other things,
She was a work of art.

Whenever it was my birthday,
The first to call each time,
Right on midnight every year,
She'd never let me down.

The night before her wedding,
Together we did stay.
Home with her parents at their house,
Dreaming of her special day.

Introducing friends to her,
My friends were hers she said.
Just ask 'bout my mate Larry,
Called her lobster, she was so red.

Salmon sandwiches at Christmas,
On a Christmas plate.
Always made with no complaint,
For my special mate.

That mate was my husband Mark,
Accepted as her own.
She took him as a nephew,
Straight into her home.

But my aunt she was primarily,
A confidante, a friend.
We shared so many secrets,
Advice that we would lend.

We had many years together,
For her since she was young.
I'd never trade a moment,
Just wish there were more…just one.

Poem 14
Up in the Sky

Serenity, floating
Up in the blue sky.
Peaceful. Retreating
From my old life.

Left that below now.
No worrying no more.
Who cares if the bills paid.
Or who fixes the door.

Who cares if the shopping's done.
Who cares whether phone rings.
Who cares who comes calling.
The serenity this brings.

Looking around now,
Blue sky all I see,
Occasional cloud
Floating, looking at me.

No one else up here,
Not even a bird,
Quiet as anything,
Not a sound to be heard.

Ignoring the world below.
Don't need to see.
Only about this world
Up here with me.

Poem 15
Just Thinking…

You used to love Christmas.
Don't get me anything you'd say,
But you'd get me the world.

I don't need anything you'd say.
But when I said that
You didn't listen.

Birthday and Christmas on the same day.
You never liked that.
You always wanted me to have two separate days.

You kept me up till midnight Christmas Eve
Every single year.
To open one present as it turned to midnight.

We always had a hotel night,
Every year for my birthday.
A gorgeous meal out too.

This year, you're not here.
I don't know how to feel.
It hurts, but memories make me smile too.

The Christmas dinner will be there.
I'm sure there'll be wine.
Maybe cake too.

But no you. Just thoughts of you.
The memories of you.
And I will smile at those.

Poem 16
Mum

You'll always be my mum,
A friend, a confidante.
The one I tell it all to.
Whether I should or not!

We always could say anything.
There were no holds barred with us.
We'd laugh, smile and talk and say
Anything we want.

I've memories shared with you and Nan.
And just with you alone.
I've memories shared with you and dad.
My memories with you are gold.

Memories are precious things.
A book you write with love.
You don't even realise you're doing it.
Those memories soar above.

Poem 17
New Year

New Year brings new promises
Of things, we plan to do.
New Year brings in thoughts.
The old year in review.

Writing a new story
From January on.
Making resolutions
Hoping they'll be strong.

What to do to celebrate
The turning of the year.
Spend it with your family,
The people you hold dear.

Don't rush out drinking too much.
Don't go out with the crowds.
Stay at home, it's peaceful
And there are less crowds.

Get up on that sofa.
Find the remote control.
Start flicking through the movies.
The rest of the day is your own.

Find a sentimental movie,
One you've seen before.
Grab a glass of wine or two.
Bring the bottle – it's the law!

Relax enjoy the quality.
Relax enjoy the fun.
Relax they're making memories.
Your life – you just have one.

Poem 18
Wizards

Martin was a wizard.
He knew a lot of spells.

He had a wand; it was made of wood.
It didn't work so well.

He tried to make his car fast.
He waved his wand a lot.

His car went slow, he didn't know
Why it stayed on the spot.

He tried to conjure cider.
Saves me going out he said.

He waved his wand and waited,
But water came instead.

The wand, he thought the problem.
Due to being made of wood.

He searched and searched, kept looking,
To find anything he could.

He went down to the wand shop,
To see what he could find.

He searched but only could find wood.
Nothing else inside.

He started to get cranky.
A little upset he was.

Nothing went his way he said.
He was getting very cross.

He went online and looked
And found just what he needed.

The type of wand, he was searching for.
No more feeling cheated.

He sent off for a new wand.
This one made of plastic.

Happy now, it's on his way,
He just felt fantastic.

The day it arrived at his house,
Excitement at fever pitch.

He pulled off the wrapping quickly,
His fingers sure did twitch.

Waved it around, without a care,
Muttered a new spell.

Thankfully for Martin,
His wand worked very well!

Poem 19
Walking Out...

Creaky trees, freaky trees,
Made me stop & stare.
Creaky trees, freaky trees,
Made me kinda scared.

Made me stop and turn,
Made me stop and stare,
Creaky trees, freaky trees,
Made me kinda scared.

The wood, the place I always go,
Always felt so safe.
Listening to all the noises,
Was getting kind of late.

I kept walking, dog with me,
Just the two of us.
Nothing really there to see,
Just the windy rush.

Leaves were dropping at our feet,
Crunching as we walked.
All the sights and sounds we hear,
There was no need to talk.

Looking at the pathway,
Looking at the lake,
Looking at the creek as well,
So many sights to take.

Got to get me going now.
Back to home I go.
Short stroll away from me,
My husband waits…I know.

Poem 20
79 Days

I sit and watch TV and look to see you there.
You're not there. I can't ask you a question.
I can't offer you a cup of tea.

I go to put washing on. You're not there.
You don't ask me to make sure your favourite top is washed.
But it's still clean and ready for you.

You aren't there next to me when I wake.
But I still wake as if you are. Turn over to see what you need.
You're not there. You don't need anything.

I wake up and wonder. Do I have to get up?
Why do I have to get up? Do I need to shower and dress?
But I do.

I realise that life has to continue. I get up, get ready.
Workout my day. Dog walk. Shopping.
Go cycling.

There still is one huge gap. A huge gap in my heart.
It will always be there, no matter what happens to me as life goes on.
No matter what, you're still missing.

I know that you loved me as much as I loved you.
I know that the life we had was as perfect as we could make it.
The ending was too soon, but it was on your terms.

I'll always love you and miss you.

Poem 21
Music

Sitting by my piano.
Tinkering on the keys.
Music book and pencil.
Thinking melodies.

I tap the keys not thinking.
But nothing ever comes.
I bang them even harder.
Imagining they're drums.

But drums they are beside me.
Back to the piano I go.
Somehow music is coming.
Inspiration starts to flow.

I write down every note.
I savour every chord.
The music keeps on coming.
A song I float towards.

Now I think of lyrics.
What to write about.
Write what you know they said to me.
Of that there is no doubt.

Poem 22
The Ocean

The sound of the ocean,
The roar of the sea,
The feel of the breeze,
It does wonders for me.

Makes me feel special,
Makes me feel alive,
Makes me feel at one with the world,
I stand on a rock, ready to dive.

Into the blue,
Into the roar,
Into the deep,
Swim out, back to shore.

Floating around,
Feeling the sea,
Wondering why,
It feels like this to me.

Relaxing and calm,
That's all I could say.
Back to the beach,
At the end of the day.

Poem 23
Reading

Picking up a book,
Did I make the right choice?
Will it interest me?

Looking at the cover,
What's the image?
Does it interest me?

Looking at the title,
What does it say?
Yes, it interests me.

Take the book home.
Settle down, kettle on.
It has grabbed me.

Lock the door.
Let no one in.
Enjoy the moment.

Poem 24
IT

It came while I was sleeping,
It came into my mind,
It came into my memories,
To see what it could find.

It came to my subconscious,
It came to take a look,
It came to try and read me,
Just like you read a book.

I don't know it came there.
I don't know why it stayed.
I don't know what it found,
But it made me afraid.

It made my breath erratic,
It made my eyes quite wide,
It made my heart race quite fast,
I could feel it from inside.

The one thing I'm quite aware of,
I don't know what it was.
I don't know if I'll ever know,
What's the odds?

Poem 25
Sleeping

Baby, when you're sleeping,
Only so much I can do.
I try hard to protect you
Of what might come for you.

Saving you from nightmares,
Saving you from dreams,
Saving you from monsters,
Save you from your fears.

I stay until you are sleeping.
Stay till your eyes are closed.
I hold on to your hand now.
I hold on to your soul.

I hold on to my memories
Of you here as a child.
I think about you growing up.
I sit here and I smile.

You'll always be my baby.
However old you are.
I'll always have my memories
Of you, my little star.

Poem 26
When Life Took a Turn

Life took a turn,
For my husband and me,
Myasthenia gravis,
The culprit you see.

Friends heard of our plight,
A ticket they got.
One person, then four,
Arrived right on the dot.

Settled into our house.
It had been a few years
Since wed been together.
Had laughs, we had tears.

Went to pay a visit
To Australia zoo.
This was the one item
They wanted to do.

Hold a koala,
That was Tracey's thing.
The others saw animals
That bite and would sting.

The rest of the time,
Relaxing we were.
Having a beer
Or just a cuppa.

Some jobs round the house
Were completed by them.
You can't buy that friendship,
It's there till the end.

Was only six days
They had here with us.
Felt so much more,
Time given with love.

Almost thirty year friends.
As true as they come.
Can never repay you.
Thank you, not enough.

Des was the best man
When we got wed.
Martin his brother,
I'll come too, he said.

Tony and Tracey,
Married they are.
Friends for years.
Good friends by far.

Thank you for coming,
All the way here,
Sharing the love,
Sharing the cheer.

Your friendship is precious.
There are no words.
What you have is priceless.
You guys are our world.

Poem 27
Why Did It Happen to Me?

I became a widow.
Why did it happen to me?

I lost my best friend.
Why did it happen to me?

I'm too young to be a widow.
Why did it happen to me?

I'm alone now.
Why did that happen to me?

Friends don't call anymore.
Why does that happen?

Everyone says "you're strong".
Why don't they see I'm not.

My life has changed, but no one sees.
Their life goes on without me.

My life is wrong now, that's just fact.
No one sees that. Huge impact.

I need my old life.
This one is wrong.

I'm sick of hearing,
   Life goes on.

Poem 28
Night Time

There are no words.
Night time falls.
It's lonely.
Here.
Just me.

No matter the time.
I try to sleep,
But
It doesn't work.
I'm awake.

Trying to sleep.
Bring on dreams.
Images.
In my head.
Of him.

He comes to me at night.
Laughs with me.
Smiles with me.
Cries with me.
In the morning, he is gone.

Poem 29
The Soldier

The soldier came home.
Years at war.
Physically able.
Mentally sore.

The things he had seen.
The things he had to do.
Can't even imagine,
The pain he'd been through.

Been out to Berlin.
Falklands as well.
Been to Northern Island.
The soldier has been through hell.

None of us know,
Unless we have been there.
We don't understand.
We're just not aware.

We can help him return
To a life, he once knew.
But it's never the same
For the soldier, the few.

Poem 30
Grief

It hurts, there's no way round it.
It hits you hard and fast.
There's nothing you can do about it.
Just hold on for the ride.

It's painful and it's frightening
If you've not known grief before.
How do you even cope?
Can you pick yourself off the floor?

Grief makes you want to curl up
And shutter out the world.
It makes you want to forget about
Everything you love the most.

Grief makes you scared of losing
Everything you care about.
It makes you hold on tightly,
Both now and all throughout.

Losing something is tragic,
But life goes on we know.
It's up to you to live it.
It's up to you to grow.

Poem 31
On the Plane

The voice called the flight,
I got up, made my way.

Walked to the gate,
Are you ready? They say.

I walked to the plane,
They showed me my seat.

For a change in first class,
They'd upgraded me!

As I sat in my chair,
Champagne in my hand.

Would could I say?
This I understand.

I can tolerate this!
All of the way.

Anything that you want,
The air stewardesses say.

The flight took off on time,
I rest in my seat.

More champagne flows
And more than I can eat.

After a sleep,
The plane lands down.

Off on my travels now,
Milling around.

Seeing the world,
Bits I've never seen.

Loving my life here,
Living the dream.

Poem 32
Nanna

I know that you miss Granddad.
I know that you still care.
I know you'll love him always.
He's with you everywhere.
He's with you when you wash your face.
He's with you when you talk.
He's with you in the garden.
He's with you when you walk.
He's with you with the children.
He's there when you're alone.
I know sometimes it's lonely.
Please pick up the phone.
You miss him when he'd whistle,
As he came down the stairs.
You miss him in the garden,
If not indoors, he'd be there.
You imagine when you're cooking
That he'll be home for tea.
Realisation sets in
And you know he'll never be.
You miss him when it's Christmas,
You miss him on birthdays too.
Trust me, he is watching.
Just you watch that rose tree bloom.

Poem 33
Parents

What can you say about parents?
That hasn't already been said.
What would you say to your parents?
What's running through your head?
Everyone needs their parents,
No matter what they say.
Everyone needs the love
That they give you every day.
A phone call or a letter,
A card or an email,
It's all it takes to make a change,
It will never fail.
Your parents give you life,
They give you a good start,
They give you all the love they can,
It comes right from the heart.
They see you through your schooling.
They see you to a job.
They see you find a partner.
They see you wander off!
Off to the new life that you make.
You spend with your new partner.
Visits home less frequent.
As your new life gets started,
Always remember your parents.
For the start you got,
Always remember your parents.
When they had nothing, you got the lot.

Poem 34
Becoming a Parent

Looking at a child,
Knowing that they depend on you now.
Looking at that child,
Can you do it? Wondering how!

Looking at that child,
They look back at you.
They look at you for answers,
To see if you are true.

You raise that child with love,
It's all that you can do.
Love them, hug them for all they're worth,
In the family, you're the glue.

You hold the world together.
You hold it with your love.
You hold it with the hugs you give
That your child is thinking of.

Being a parent is special,
A joy not had by all.
Treasure every moment,
No matter how big or small.

Your child is a gift to be treasured
By you and your family.
A child is a gift to be treasured,
Live quite happily.

Poem 35
102 Days

102 days since you've been gone.
The time has gone fast,
Feels like years.

I am looking for you at home.
Look for you when I'm out.
I look to get you clothes when I see something nice.

You're still so present to me.
Don't think you'll ever go.
I hope not.

I feel you in my memories.
I see you in my dreams.
Still so present to me.

I feel you in the bedroom
As I lay there thinking,
Still so present to me.

I feel you everywhere.
I turn to you, but you're not there.
Still present in my mind to me.

I loved every moment in life with you.
Thank you for every moment of life with you.
Love you every day now and always.